Mama Rex & T

The Reading Champion

by Rachel Vail

illustrations by Steve Björkman

ORCHARD BOOKS
An Imprint of Scholastic Inc.
New York

For Liza and Aimee, who are both absolute champions.
—*RV*

For Alex Uhl, who helps kids read.
—*SB*

Text copyright © 2003 by Rachel Vail.
Illustrations copyright © 2003 by Steve Björkman.

Library of Congress-in-Publication Data available.
ISBN 0-439-47193-1

10 9 8 7 6 5 4 3   03 04 05 06 07

Book design by Elizabeth Parisi

Printed in the U.S.A.
First Scholastic edition, April 2003

Contents

Chapter 1
A JUMBLE OF LETTERS

T sat at the reading table with Mrs. Sudak.

"You can do it, T," said Mrs. Sudak. "Just concentrate."

T tried to concentrate. He looked down at the page in front of him.

CRASH! Over in the blocks area, a castle had collapsed. T's best friend, Walter, stamped his foot.

"Bleh!" shouted Walter. "T, look!"

T and Walter had spent all morning building that castle. They had even included a trapdoor and a dungeon.

Now it was ruined.

Veronica and Malcolm started helping Walter with the repair work.

"T," said Mrs. Sudak.

T looked again at the page. It was full of
letters. Mrs. Sudak was waiting for T to make
words out of the big jumble of letters.

T scratched an itch on his arm.

Some giggling sounds from the other side of the room made T turn around. Ariel and Gemma were leaning close together. T noticed that they were glancing over at him.

T clonked his head down on the table.

"They're laughing at me," he whispered.

"No," said Mrs. Sudak. "They're looking at me — to see if I noticed that they spilled the purple paint all over their feet."

T peeked at their feet. "Oh," he said.

Mrs. Sudak pointed at the page. "What does this say, T?"

"I don't know," said T. He looked out the window and wished he could be under the tree.

"It might help if you look at the word," whispered Mrs. Sudak.

T glanced at it and guessed, "*Pickle?*"
"No," said Mrs. Sudak.
T guessed again. "*Absolutely?*"
Mrs. Sudak pointed at the book. "This word here."
"*Flabbergasted? Knees? Orangutan?*"
Mrs. Sudak looked confused.

"See? It doesn't help to look." T clonked his head down again. "Can I go play blocks now?"

Mrs. Sudak whispered, "I'm going to let you in on my secret trick."

T peeked up.

"It's called Magic Boxes," said Mrs. Sudak. "You're good at clues, right?"

T nodded a little. He and Walter played Deep Detectives almost every day.

"Look!" Mrs. Sudak shrieked. "A clue! In the Magic Box!"

T looked. The Magic Box was just Mrs. Sudak's fingers. They covered up almost the whole page — all but one letter.

"That's not a clue," said T. "That's an *F*."

"Aha!" yelled Mrs. Sudak. "And what sound does an *F* make?"

T made the *F* sound, then glanced across the room.

Walter had given up on rebuilding and was flopped on the floor, reading a big, thick book. Walter was a Reading Champion.

T slumped down in his chair.

"Another clue," whispered Mrs. Sudak. "This is a toughie."

T glanced down. "It's an *A*," he said. "What's so tough about that?"

"Hmm," said Mrs. Sudak.
She moved the Magic Box until another letter appeared.
He smiled. "That's my favorite," he said. "*T*."

"Now put the sounds together," whispered Mrs. Sudak.

"Then can I go back to the blocks area?" asked T.

Mrs. Sudak nodded, so T tried.

"Ffff – aaaa – T. Fffff-aaaa-t. Fat. Fat. Fat."

"Well, I've been trying to eat fewer doughnuts," said Mrs. Sudak.

T smiled. "I read *fat*?"

"You put the clues together and figured it out," said Mrs. Sudak.

"Yeah," said T. "I guess I did."

"You can go play now if you want."

"Great." T stood up to go. "Mrs. Sudak? How many words are there?"

"In the world?" asked Mrs. Sudak. "I don't know. Thousands and thousands."

"Oh," said T. "And I can read a grand total of one of them." He trudged away, toward the blocks.

Chapter 2
STINKY AND GREAT

After school, Mama Rex asked, "What did you learn in school today?"

"I learned to read," said T.

"Really?" asked Mama Rex.

"Yes," said T. "I can read the word FAT."

"Oh," said Mama Rex. "OK."

"Let me know if you need me to read it," offered T. "Any time."

Mama Rex and T walked along for a while, window-shopping. Mama Rex said, "I have to get my nails done. Want to come? "

"Yuck," said T. "It's stinky in there."

They looked in the window of a bookstore. "Hey," said Mama Rex. "How about if I buy you a book, and you can read while I get my nails done?"

"OK," said T. "But it will have to be a book with the word FAT in it."

Mama Rex and T went into the bookstore. "Hello," said Mama Rex to the man behind the counter. "Do you have a good book for a young dinosaur who knows how to read the word FAT?"

The man scratched his chin. He looked at the ceiling. T looked at the ceiling, too. There was nothing there.

"Yes," said the man, and he dashed away.

Mama Rex and T waited. In two seconds, the man was back with a book, which he handed to T.

"FAT!" yelled T, pointing at the word he knew how to read.

"We'll take it," said Mama Rex.

    T carried the bag with the book inside it to
the nail place. T sat down next to Mama Rex's
foot and pulled out his new book.
    There was a word after *FAT*. T looked at each
letter, one at a time. *C – A – T*. *CAT*, read T.
FAT CAT.
    T smiled. It sounded like a good book. He
opened it and flipped through the pages, looking
at the pictures and listening to the voices of the
grown-ups above him.

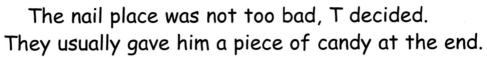

The nail place was not too bad, T decided. They usually gave him a piece of candy at the end.

T looked down at his book again. There were a lot of letters on the page. T tried to get his fingers to make a Magic Box. It didn't work as nicely as Mrs. Sudak's, but he kept trying.

P-A-T, read T. *PAT.*

PAT SAT.

PAT SAT ON A FAT CAT.

SPLAT!

T laughed.

"Having fun?" asked Mama Rex from up above him.

"Yeah," said T, and he kept going.

"DRAT!" YELLED PAT.

"A FLAT CAT!"

T laughed so hard that he bumped into the nail table.

Mama Rex bent down. "What are you doing?"

T tried to catch his breath. "Pat!"

"Pat?" asked Mama Rex.

The nail polisher and Mama Rex shrugged at each other.

"Pat splatted the cat!" yelled T.

He stood up and showed Mama Rex the book. He read the words to her, then turned the page and slowly read:

"I AM A CAT," YELLED THE FLAT FAT CAT. "NOT A MAT!"

T laughed so hard that he fell down.

"T," said Mama Rex. "I think..."
T stopped laughing. "What?"
"I think you know how to read," she said.

T blinked a few times, and then he looked back at his book. Nobody had read the story to him. He had figured it out for himself. The letters had become — words.

T nodded. "I can read." He smiled.

Mama Rex grabbed T and picked him up.
"Hooray for you!" she shouted.

Mama Rex twirled T around and around the
nail place.

Her nail polish was ruined, but she didn't even care.

"I can read!" T yelled. "I — am a Reading
Champion!"

Chapter 3
SWEET DREAMS

Mama Rex tucked T into bed. "Have sweet dreams," said Mama Rex.

"I will," said T.

"Ouch," said Mama Rex.

She reached under the blanket. A book.

She smiled and pulled it out, and then she tried to tuck T in again.

"Sweet dre — ouch!"

She pulled out another book.

She tucked him in a third time.

"Sweet — ouch!" she yelled.

Mama Rex picked up T's blanket. She looked underneath. She saw T and a whole mountain range of books surrounding him.

"T!" said Mama Rex.

T smiled. "I wish the whole world were made of books."

"Your whole bed is," said Mama Rex. "How are you going to sleep?"

"I don't think I can," said T. "I'm too excited. I want to read everything in the entire universe."

Mama Rex smiled back at T. "I know the feeling," she whispered. "But you can't do it all tonight."

"Aw," moaned T.

Mama Rex cleared a wide alley between the stacks of books.

She climbed into T's bed beside him.

"But," she said, "you can start."

T grinned. "Want me to read you something?"

"Yes," said Mama Rex. "I sure do."

"I'm not great at it yet," warned T. "I might need some help."

"That's why I'm here," whispered Mama Rex.

Bedtime sailed by.
Mama Rex and T didn't notice.
They were reading, quietly, together.